# Thomas A. Edison

Jennifer Strand

**abdopublishing.com**

Published by Abdo Zoom™, PO Box 398166, Minneapolis, Minnesota 55439. Copyright © 2017 by Abdo Consulting Group, Inc. International copyrights reserved in all countries. No part of this book may be reproduced in any form without written permission from the publisher. Abdo Zoom™ is a trademark and logo of Abdo Consulting Group, Inc.

Printed in the United States of America, North Mankato, Minnesota
072016
092016

THIS BOOK CONTAINS RECYCLED MATERIALS

Cover Photo: Corbis
Interior Photos: Corbis, 1; Library of Congress, 4, 8, 13, 14; Everett - Art/Shutterstock Images, 5; Joseph Sohn/Shutterstock Images, 6; Frank Lewis Dyer, 7; Oleg Golovnev/Shutterstock Images, 9; North Wind Picture Archives, 10, 11, 15; Everett Historical/Shutterstock Images, 12, 16–17; Detroit Publishing Co./Library of Congress, 18; AP Images, 19

Editor: Emily Temple
Series Designer: Madeline Berger
Art Direction: Dorothy Toth

**Publisher's Cataloging-in-Publication Data**
Names: Strand, Jennifer, author.
Title: Thomas A. Edison / by Jennifer Strand.
Description: Minneapolis, MN : Abdo Zoom, [2017] | Series: Incredible inventors | Includes bibliographical references and index.
Identifiers: LCCN 2016941396 | ISBN 9781680792317 (lib. bdg.) | ISBN 9781680793994 (ebook) | 9781680794885 (Read-to-me ebook)
Subjects: LCSH: Edison, Thomas A. (Thomas Alva), 1847-1931--Juvenile literature. | Inventors--United States--Biography--Juvenile literature. | Electrical engineers--United States--Biography--Juvenile literature. | Scientists--United States--Biography--Juvenile literature. | Menlo Park (N.J.)--History--Juvenile literature.
Classification: DDC 621.3092 [B]--dc23
LC record available at http://lccn.loc.gov/2016941396

# Table of Contents

# Introduction

Thomas A. Edison was an inventor.

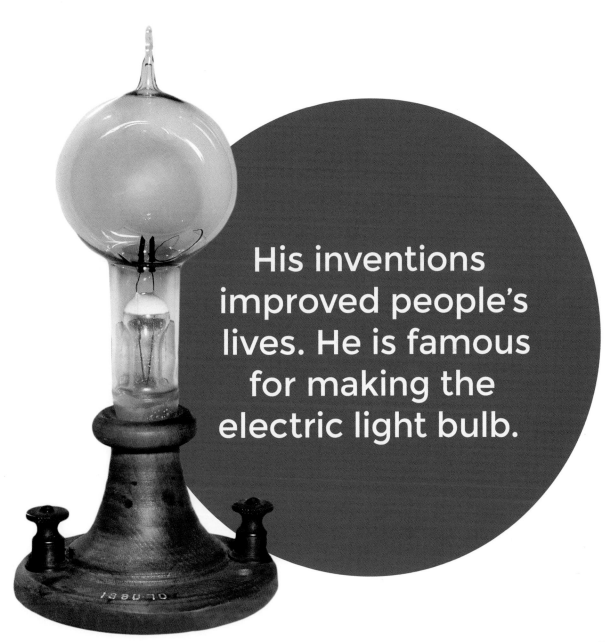

His inventions improved people's lives. He is famous for making the electric light bulb.

5

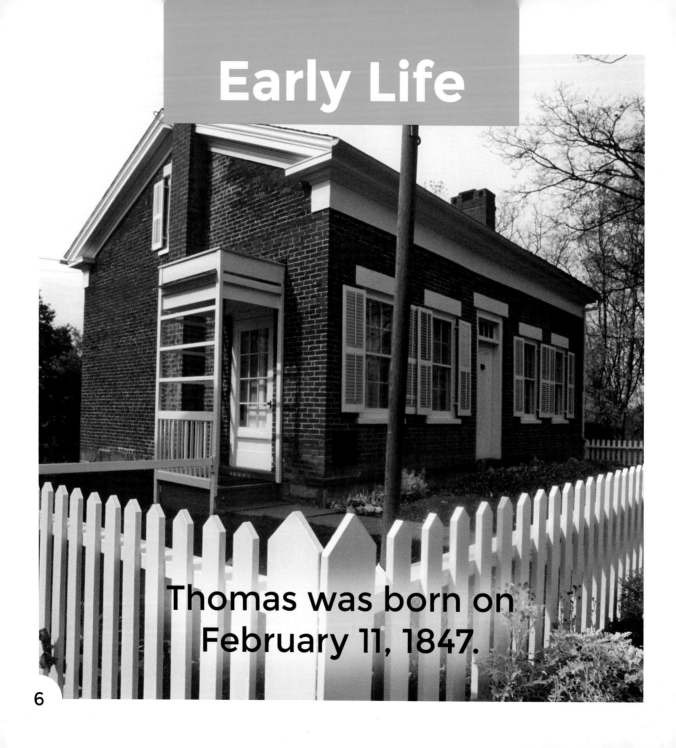

# Early Life

Thomas was born on February 11, 1847.

His mother taught him. He liked to read and do **experiments**.

At age 15 Thomas
started a business.
He made a newspaper.

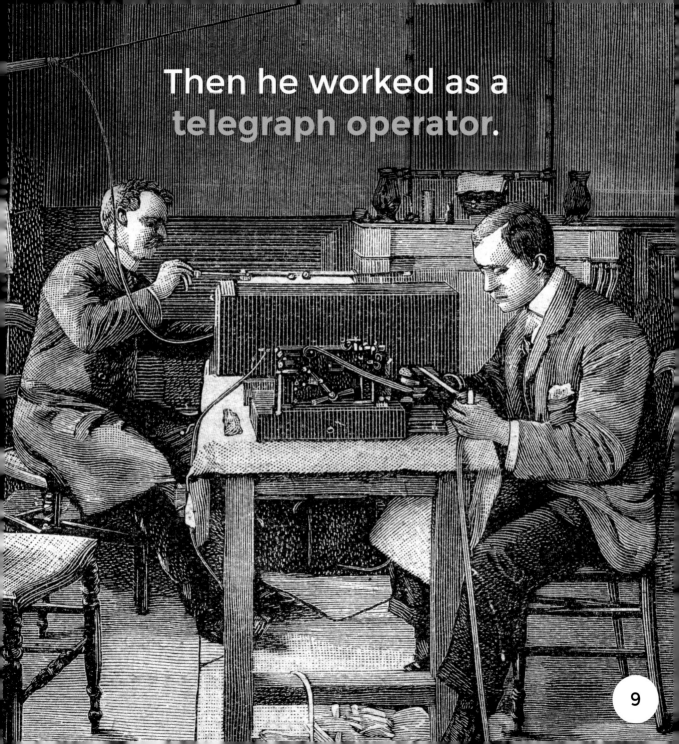

Then he worked as a telegraph operator.

9

Leader

Edison began inventing.

He created new kinds of telegraphs. Many people bought them.

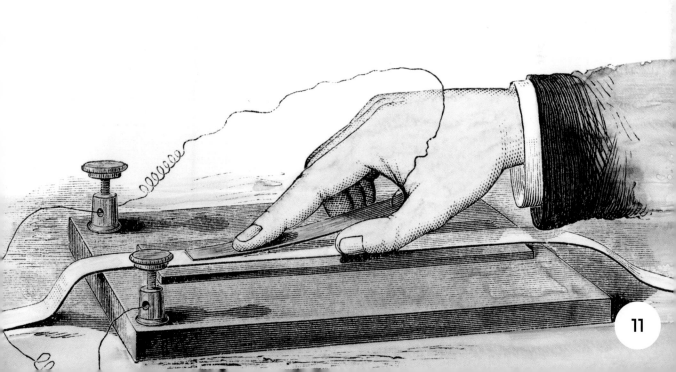

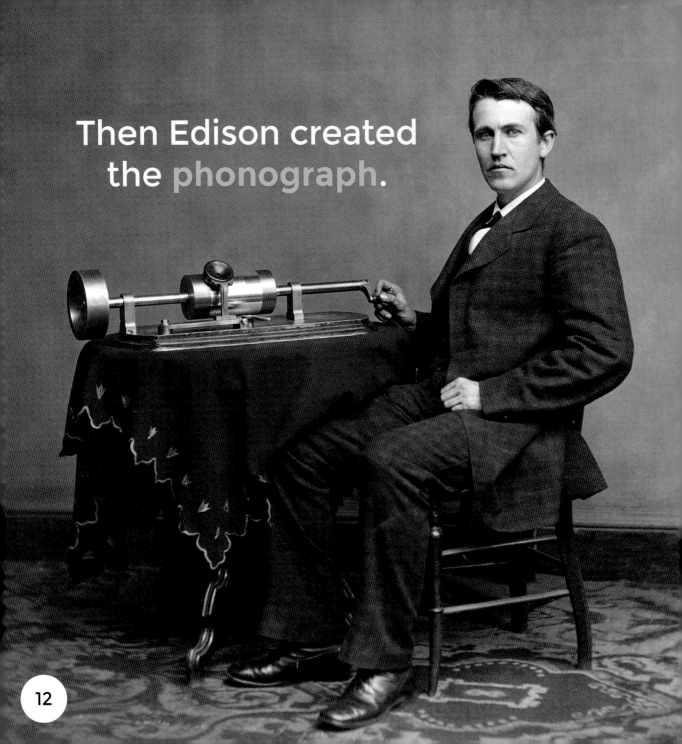

Then Edison created the **phonograph.**

It played sound recordings.
This made him famous.

Homes were lit with lamps.
The lamps used oil or gas.

# Edison made the first electric light bulb.
# It changed daily life.

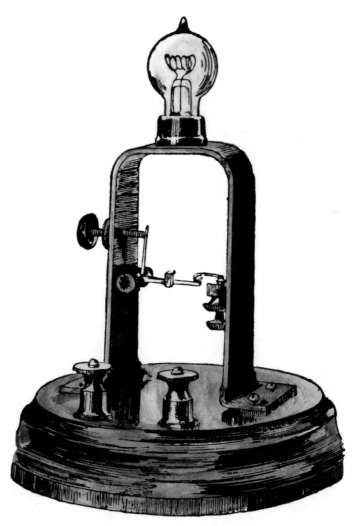

Edison built
an electric
power station.
It sent power and
light to part of
New York City.

# Legacy

Edison died in 1931.
He held 2,332 **patents**.

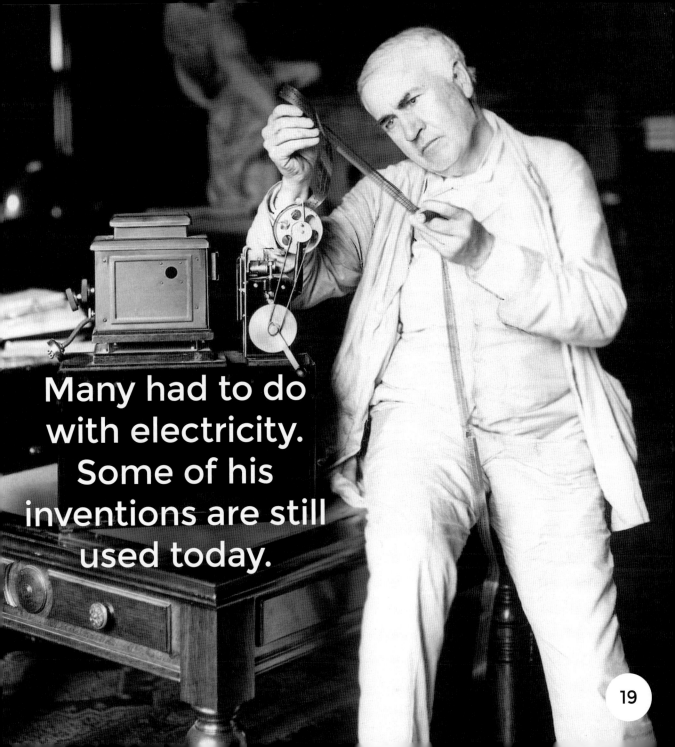

Many had to do with electricity. Some of his inventions are still used today.

# Thomas A. Edison

**Born:** February 11, 1847

**Birthplace:** Milan, Ohio

**Wives:** Mary Stilwell (died); Mina Miller

**Known For:** Edison invented many things, including the phonograph and the electric light bulb.

**Died:** October 18, 1931

# Key Dates

**1847:** Thomas Alva Edison is born on February 11.

**1863:** Edison begins work as a telegraph operator.

**1877:** Edison invents the phonograph.

**1879:** Edison creates the electric light bulb.

**1891:** Edison and a partner invent a movie camera.

**1931:** Edison dies on October 18.

# Glossary

**experiment** - a scientific test.

**operator** - someone whose job is to run a machine.

**patent** - an official document giving one person the right to make, use, or sell an invention.

**phonograph** - a machine that plays sounds from a record.

**telegraph** - a machine that carries coded messages over wires.

# Booklinks

For more information
on **Thomas A. Edison**, please visit
booklinks.abdopublishing.com

## Z**○○**m In on Biographies!

Learn even more with the Abdo Zoom
Biographies database. Check out
**abdozoom.com** for more information.

# Index